First World War
and Army of Occupation
War Diary
France, Belgium and Germany

40 DIVISION
Divisional Troops
185 Brigade Royal Field Artillery
4 June 1916 - 31 August 1916

WO95/2599/1

The Naval & Military Press Ltd
www.nmarchive.com
Published in association with The National Archives

Published by

The Naval & Military Press Ltd

Unit 10 Ridgewood Industrial Park,

Uckfield, East Sussex,

TN22 5QE England

Tel: +44 (0) 1825 749494

www.naval-military-press.com

www.nmarchive.com

This diary has been reprinted in facsimile from the original. Any imperfections are inevitably reproduced and the quality may fall short of modern type and cartographic standards.

© **Crown Copyright**
Images reproduced by permission of The National Archives, London, England, 2015.

Contents

Document type	Place/Title	Date From	Date To
Heading	WO95/2599/1		
Heading	40th Division 185th Brigade R.F.A 16 Jun 1916 Aug Broken Up		
War Diary	Havre	04/06/1916	04/06/1916
War Diary	H.Q. Vermelles A. Vermelles B & C Annequin D. From No 7	02/07/1916	03/07/1916
War Diary	H.Q. Les Brebis	04/07/1916	18/07/1916
War Diary	Les Brebis	04/07/1916	07/07/1916
War Diary	Les Brebis	01/08/1916	31/08/1916

W005/25991/1

40TH DIVISION

185TH BRIGADE R.F.A.

~~JUN 1916~~

16 JUN – 1916 AUG

BROKEN UP

WAR DIARY

of 185 Bde. R.F.A.

INTELLIGENCE SUMMARY
(Erase heading not required.)

Army Form C. 2118

ORIGINAL

June 1916.

Instructions regarding War Diaries and Intelligence Summaries are contained in F.S. Regs., Part II. and the Staff Manual respectively. Title Pages will be prepared in manuscript.

June 16 only

Place	Date	Hour	Summary of Events and Information	Remarks and references to Appendices
Le HAVRE	June 4		All 4 Batteries & H.Q. landed at HAVRE off S.S. "Anvardyk" & "C.s.t. le line" "African Prince" & 10 AM & stayed 1 day at the night at No 5 Dock Rest Camp. The following officers accompanied their Batteries. H.Q. Col. D. Cawdley - Wilmot - Cmdg. Maj. G. C. L. Thornton D.S.O. Capt. R. Pilcherick - Adj. Maj. J. H. Pike - Cmdg. Maj. C. W. Gill Lt. A. E. Arcuthers - Adj. 1/& Capt. G. A. Newton 2/&. J. M. D. Humphreys 2/&. H. D. Gibson Lt. W. Campbell 2/&. R. A. Spencer - O.O. C. A. Ralph Smith " J. M. G. Cook " L. W. Baker 2/&. A. B. Boone R. C. M. Alexander - R.F.A. " Cr. M. C. Carleton " A. E. Donne " J. M. Bell Granville Chapp. Lt. W. Ramsden - R.A.M.C. " M. A. D. Dellaykaye " S. W. R. Preston W. Kenny Pymen-Jones Ct. A. W. Bennison - A.V.C.	
TRAIN	5		All Batteries left HAVRE by Train during the day	
AMES	6		Batteries detrained at BERGETTE & LILLERS - marched to AMES about 10 Miles.	
"	7/6		Remained at AMES, 4 N.C.Os came to us from the Bde. about 3 p.m. Half of Batteries & half H.Q. marched to billets at [?] from 12. 5 Division on Vermelles front - 15" Div. D/185 moved to 18. Div. - MOEUX les MINES, - H.Q. to Regt.HQ Group - Philosophe - B & C left Group - 2 Battery and at BARLEQUIN.	
PHILOSOPHE				
1 Vermilles	13		Very wet day. The remainder of H.Q. A & D. Batteries came up from AMES - The 15" Div. R relieve Irish Div. June 14. Portion of Rapid Group way flares inside Hay Thornton away April 15.	
2 MOEUX W- MINES	14		B. & C. Batteries were round templed, Batteries up in at AIX NOULETTE Redan D/185 also in the line. 40th Division & 5th Division. Reason Division to 1st Corps. Batteries in action other than usual supply of group Commander	
	15		Remained in station, command to Division in which Batteries took part, under orders of Group Commander. June - Bombarded par. BORA on this front has cancelled from nearly wind.	
			At 3 AM cartrine Present in Quarries and shelled considerable around Chesny. C.O. and went to reconnoitre artillery positions in NOTRE DAM in neighborhood of CANTLAIN. Usually wet day. Rifles Batty on the 4th Corps very wet day.	
			Cloudy cold - A.R.C. Batteries impossed in building a building M.G. with a sweeping in Maisbrystell. D. Cawdley - Wilmot Col. Cmdg. 185 Bde. R.F.A.

This diary was attached to portfolio
b. 16th - 16 June

Original
July Sht 1.

40/ of July
Army Form C. 2118
185 R.F.A.
July 1916
VOL 2

WAR DIARY
of 185, Bde, R.F.A.
INTELLIGENCE SUMMARY
(Erase heading not required.)

Instructions regarding War Diaries and Intelligence Summaries are contained in F.S. Regs, Part II. and the Staff Manual respectively. Title Pages will be prepared in manuscript.

Place	Date July	Hour	Summary of Events and Information	Remarks and references to Appendices
H.Q. VERMELLES A. Vermelles B) Annequin D. Fouquière?	2		Fine. Received Orders that the guns of the 40th Div. were to relieve those of the 1st Div. on the Right of the 1st Corps.	
	3		Fine. At 10 p.m. the Div. Artillery commenced to withdraw its guns - to replace those of the 1st Division in the MAROC & CALONNE Fronts.	
H.Q. LES BREBIS	4		The withdrawal was completed at 10 p.m. & the 1st Division was replaced by 40th Divn.	
"	5		H.Q. 185. Bde. R.F.A. moved to Les Brebis. A Battery was split up & attached to Left Group - (MAROC) under Lt Colonel Holmes Wilson - 188 Arty. B. " " " " " " " " " " C. " " Right Group - (CALONNE) " Lt Colonel Gill - 178 Bd. D. " " " " " " " " " " " Right Group (") " Right Group (") one Gun - Left Group. 3 guns.	
"	6		Very wet afternoon.	
"	7		Fine, but wet wind.	
"	8		Cloudy & wet. Fine Later - Am? was very much restricted to that was not much taking place	
"	9		Fine.	
"	10		Fine - cold N. wind	
"	11		Fine. Cloudy & cold. 2 Lts. Selby, Munvey, Ord, Giblin posted to the Brigade - 2nd Lt. Pepper Jones - Doloday posted	
"	12		Fine. Cloudy. to French Mortar Batteries.	
"	13		Very dull - 2/Lt Henry posted to V. Battery T.M. 40th Div.	
"	14		Cloudy & dull.	
"	15		Fine - C. Battery sent to 39th Div. to form a group S. of La Bassée Canal. Took up a position at ANNEQUIN. Group Commander Lt. Col. Christie, R.F.M.	
"	16		Fine. cloudy. Very little Am? expended on this front. Rain after 2 p.m.	
"	17		Very thick mist + drizzle	
"	18		Fine but dull.	

Original
Sheet 2. July 1916

Army Form C. 2118

WAR DIARY
of 185. Brigade. R.F.A.
INTELLIGENCE SUMMARY
(Erase heading not required.)

Instructions regarding War Diaries and Intelligence Summaries are contained in F. S. Regs, Part II. and the Staff Manual respectively. Title Pages will be prepared in manuscript.

Place	Date	Hour	Summary of Events and Information	Remarks and references to Appendices
LES BREBIS	July 19		Mainly dull - fine later.	
	20		Mainly but fine. Very heavy firing from "Aubers Ridge" direction.	
	21		Fine - Mainly.	
	22		Very mainly. Dull all day. Orders came for re-distribution of H.Q. Div. Artillery on this front owing to 15th Div. being withdrawn. The 16th Div. extended N. & to 40° & to took over the ground N. that the 16th Div. vacated. Made a new Sub-Group to the left, group under 2nd Lt. Robertson 1 Pl. Rode. The 185th Rode remained Brokenup & scattered.	
			Right Group: 2nd Lt. Gill 16/1855 B/181 - 2 guns D/185 - 178 Rode. anyford.	
			Left Group: 2nd Lt. Robertson Wilson - B/182 C/182 D/185- B/186 A/181 A/185 - 2 guns D/185	
			Lt Sub Group: 2nd Lt. Robertson - B/181 B/181 C/185 A/185	
	23		Dull & cold - C/185 returned to the Division after its temporary absence.	
	24		Dull & colder.	
	25		Fine but dull.	
	26		Very Mainly - but no rain - dull all day	
	27		Very wet morn. but our 2am. cleared all day.	
	28		Very damp & mainly till 11 am.	
	29		Very Damp & mainly but very hot later. 2/Lt. HENRY to W/T.M. B.A.C. no duty	
	30		Very damp & mainly - very hot later.	
	31		No cloud, very hot all day.	

R. Sandbey-Wilmot
Lt Col
Comg. 185. Bde R.F.A.

Army Form C. 2118

Vol 3

WAR DIARY
of 185 Bde, R.F.A.
INTELLIGENCE SUMMARY
(Erase heading not required.)

Sheet No 1. Aug. 1916

Instructions regarding War Diaries and Intelligence Summaries are contained in F.S. Regs., Part II. and the Staff Manual respectively. Title Pages will be prepared in manuscript.

Place	Date	Hour	Summary of Events and Information	Remarks and references to Appendices
LES BREBIS	Aug 1		Misty, very hot later. The 185 Bde. was divided up amongst the Right & Left sub-groups of CALONNE & LOOS Sectors, no one sitting in a complete unit. All tactical questions & returns on Ammunition etc. being referred to group commanders concerned.	
	2		Very hot all day	
	3		Very hot day	
	4		Very cloudy up to midday. Fine evening	
	5		Heb. Clouded up rapidly. 2nd Lieut C. Pretty seriously wounded by shell in open dug out. Majr Hill took control of the battery. Lieut Carter - Major Rice coming C. Battery Pos. coming of C. & att. temporarily.	
	6		Fine. Capt Peareham 3 Battery 4.5" Bde 8" Bat sent to take over command of C.B. att. temporarily.	
	7		Cloudy	
	8		Fine. First 5 sections moved back into positions of July 3rd —	
	9		Fine. Move into positions of July 3rd completed.	
	10		Fine. Cloudy, inclined to rain by 10/77 days.	
	11		Dull & Cloudy.	
	12		Very misty morning. Very hot later.	
	13		Very hot all day.	
	14		Cloudy. Rained heavily in the afternoon but cleared in the evening.	
	15		Fine morning. Heavy showers midday. Les Brebis rather heavily shelled in the evening.	
	16		Fine all day.	
	17		Fine in the morning. Very heavy showers in the afternoon.	
	18		Very misty.	
	19		Col. A Bradley, whilst listed to 179 "Bde R.F.A. 39 "Divn." The 185 Bde. was permanently split up amongst the 178, 181 & 188 Bdes. to bring these latter to 6-gun battery establishment. One section A/185 was sent to A/181. One section A/185 to C/181. One section B/185 to A/178. One section C/185 to B/178, one section One section B/185 to B/181. One section C/185 to C/181. Capt Blewitt D.S.O. to command B/181. C/185 to C/178. Majr. Thornton D.S.O. sent to command C/181. Capt Blewitt D.S.O. to command C/188. Capt Buchan to command A/188. D/185 (Major Hill Comdg) became C/188. The remaining officers of the 185/Bde were posted to other batteries on the 40th Divn.	
	31			

1875 Wt. W593/826 1,000,000 4/15 J.B.C. & A. A.D.S.S./Forms/C. 2118.